# National Religion

A Presbyterian Political Manifesto

# National Religion

## A Presbyterian Political Manifesto

by Michael Wagner

LANDMARK
PROJECT &
*P R E S S*

*Remove not the ancient landmark...*

Printed by Landmark Project Press
*A complete e-text version is also available
on the Landmark Project website.*

Landmark Project Press
Edmonton, Canada
www.landmarkproject.net
press@landmarkproject.net

ISBN 978-0-9780987-3-5

*To W. J. Mencarow*

# CONTENTS

# Citations

The system used for citations in this book follows the *Style Manual for Political Science* published by the American Political Science Association (1993). In the text of the book, a citation includes the last name of the cited author, followed by the date of his work, and then the page number or numbers used. To find the title of the work cited, go to the *References* section at the end of the book. Locate the author's last name and the date that corresponds to the one in the citation, and you will find the specific work cited. For example, the citation "(M'Crie [1821] 1989, 162)" refers to page 162 in M'Crie's book *Unity of the Church* which was originally published in 1821, and republished in 1989. Where the author's name is not between the citation brackets, his name had just been referred to previously in the text and should therefore be obvious.

# PREFACE

This little book was originally written in 1995. At that time I had just become convinced that the position on civil government embodied in the original *Westminster Confession of Faith* was the true, Biblical position. I hoped the line of reasoning that convinced me would be helpful for others as well. So I wrote out that reasoning as it appears here.

In the early 1990s I was heavily influenced by the Christian Reconstruction movement. This book reflects that influence, especially in the sources that are quoted. However, I think that even for those who are unfavorable to Christian Reconstruction, and its theology of ethics called "theonomy," much of the argumentation can still be persuasive.

Since it first appeared (in a cheap photocopy format), the *Presbyterian Political Manifesto* has received very little attention. It has had no discernable effect on thinking about civil government among conservative Christians. Thus it has certainly failed in its primary task.

Why, then, should it be published in a regular book format? As a Presbyterian postmillennialist, I believe

that at some point in the future the original Presbyterianism of the *Westminster Confession of Faith* will
become the dominant religion right across the world.
The view of civil government taught in the *Confession*, commonly called the Establishment Principle,
will then be a common form of government. It's my
hope that this book will be helpful to some people,
convincing them that the Establishment Principle is
Biblical.

I would like to thank Jordan Dohms for his willing-
ness to add this item to the growing body of literature
that he is publishing. May Landmark Project Press be
mightily blessed of God in contributing to the revival
of Biblical Christianity leading to the coming millen-
nium.

Michael Wagner
*Edmonton, Alberta*
*December 2007*

# CHAPTER ONE

## INTRODUCTION

For the last two decades or so there has been an apparent increase in the amount of conservative Christian political activism in North America. Many evangelicals and fundamentalists who had previously shunned politics began to see the necessity of political participation in order to prevent the encroachment of the state upon their legitimate activities, such as Christian education, or to prevent national sins, such as legalized abortion.

Undoubtedly, this Christian political activity is a positive development in Canada and the United States. More Christians are taking their biblical social responsibilities seriously. But Christian political activism also raises important questions. Is the ultimate political goal of Christians simply to achieve certain conservative government policies, or is something more needed for a completely biblical agenda? Every true Christian can agree on policy outcomes such as eliminating abortion, stopping the homosexual agenda, and protecting parental rights in education, but is that all we can gather from the Scriptures as to God's will for civil government?

The learned men who wrote the *Westminster Confession of Faith* spelled out the basic biblical position on civil government. The "civil magistrate" (i.e., any power-wielding government official such as an elected politician or an unelected judge) is a minister of God (Romans 13:4). He must reward good and punish evil. How is such a person to distinguish "good" from "evil"? By God's authoritative Word, the Bible. Government officials must rule in accordance with the Bible. To put it in different words, Christianity must be the *established* religion of any society that wants to please God.

But to say that God requires societies to be governed according to the Bible raises further questions. Who should interpret the Bible for the civil authorities? Many different groups of conservative Christians have irreconcilable interpretations of the Bible. For example, some professing Christians are completely opposed to capital punishment for any crime, whereas others support it as the just punishment for not only murder, but other crimes as well. Which interpretation is true?

In order to resolve this problem a Christian state must be more than Christian in a broad sense of endorsing a general concept of biblical Christianity. It must be Christian in a specific sense; it must have a confession of faith that sets out its theological understanding of the Scriptures and how to interpret them.

It is this author's settled conviction that the *Westminster Confession of Faith* is the most accurate and thoroughgoing account of the doctrines of God's inerrant Word, and is therefore the most reasonable choice for a Christian state to adopt. It is the contention of this book that the historic Presbyterian view of the necessity for the establishment of Presbyterianism as the official religion of every society is the Scriptural view, and it is the task of this book to demonstrate that truth to the current generation of Christians.

# CHAPTER TWO

## ESTABLISHED RELIGION:
## AN INESCAPABLE CONCEPT

For most modern North Americans it seems that "religion" is looked upon as some sort of a hobby in which one may or may not participate at his leisure. Many would view themselves as having little or nothing to do with religion. "Religion is something in which other people are involved as a private endeavour. It is mostly harmless as long as it remains a private matter." But if people are openly motivated by religious concerns in their public affairs, politics in particular, religion is then thought to have intruded into a "secular" area from which it should be forbidden.

This view, however, displays a marked ignorance of what religion really is. The term "religion," in its most meaningful sense, actually refers to the underlying beliefs that everyone has about the meaning of life. In this way it is clear that all people hold to some form of religion. Paul Marshall has explained it well.

> Religion refers to the deepest commitment and deepest identity of a person or group. Hence, the

> opinion that one may discuss constitutions, politics, education, or sex without any reference to God is as much a religious view as the opinion that we are responsible to God in all we do. An expanded concept of religion allows us to take account of the fact that our lives reflect and are rooted in a particular view of the meaning of life: of the nature of society; of what human beings really are; and of their essential responsibilities, whether to self, society, or another source (1992, 6).

Thus religion is an inescapable aspect of life. Everyone has a religious viewpoint whether they acknowledge it or not. Man is a religious being.

The fact that man is a religious being is very significant for politics and government. Every aspect of life is infused with religious meaning. Each person's views about the origin and purpose of government are fundamentally based on some religious perspective. Human societies are characterized by a common religious foundation which provides cohesion and a basis for law. R.J. Rushdoony has done much to bring this to light.

> Every state is a law order, and every law order represents an enacted morality, with procedures for the enforcement of that morality. Every morality represents a form of theological order, i.e., is an aspect and expression of a religion. The church thus is not the

only religious institution; the state also is a religious institution (1986, 7).

It is very important to understand, as Rushdoony points out, "that in any culture *the source of law is the god of that society*" (1973, 4). This is closely related to the fact that "[b]ecause law governs man and society, because it establishes and declares the meaning of justice and righteousness, law is inescapably religious, in that it establishes in practical fashion the ultimate concern of a culture" (Rushdoony 1973, 4). It is clear, then, that not only is religion relevant for issues of law, politics, and government, but it cannot be separated from them. Every society has a religious basis, and cannot exist without that specific religious basis. "Since the foundations of law are inescapably religious, no society exists without a religious foundation or without a law-system which codifies the morality of its religion" (Rushdoony 1973, 5).

The result of this significant insight is that "every state or social order is a religious establishment" (Rushdoony 1986, 7). In other words, "no disestablishment of religion as such is possible in any society" (Rushdoony 1973, 5). Hence the question is never "Should we have an established religion, or not?"; rather, the question must be "Which religion should be the established religion?" We cannot escape the fact that our society, and every other society, has always had, and will always have, an established religion, whether implicitly or explicitly. The liberty and prosperity that we still (decreasingly) enjoy are residuals from an implicit Christian foundation that is quickly being eroded and replaced by the religion of secular humanism.

Once it has been demonstrated that every society has an established religion, it should not be necessary to ask any Bible-believing Christian which religion should be established. Obviously Christianity is the only acceptable choice because it is the only true religion. Since as Christians we are to be honest, there is no reason why we should shy away from being explicit about the necessity of a Christian establishment. However, since there are so many sects that go by the term "Christianity," we need to define the "brand" of Christianity that is to be established. Our society cannot rest on an ambiguous concept of Christianity. As Rushdoony, again, writes, "[e]very social order rests on a creed . . . The life of a society is its creed" (1968, 219). Thus a creed giving the best expression of the Christian faith is an indispensable document for an explicit establishment of Biblical Christianity.

The idea of having a creed that is very specific and well-defined in terms of the type of Christianity it expresses sounds very narrow and exclusive, and it is. Assuming it is a very Biblical creed, such as the *Westminster Confession of Faith*, it excludes all erroneous and heretical conceptions of Christianity. This is important with regards to political matters. By having a general and ambiguous creed, it would be less clear how God's Law is to be interpreted for application in the social and political realm. If a dispensational interpretation of the Law was accepted by the state, virtually all of the benefits of having a Christian establishment would be nullified. Other theological persuasions would also be disastrous for a true Christian state. With the *Westminster Confession of Faith* as a guide to interpreting the Scriptures, the civil authorities would be able to act according to the will of God in political matters, rather than according to the subjective opinions of men.

The *Westminster Confession of Faith* is completely Biblical. "For fidelity to Scripture, for 'logical fearlessness and power,' for 'theological comprehensiveness, and intellectual grandeur,' it is second to none" (Tallach 1980). Unfortunately, this book is not the place to go into a comparative Biblical analysis of various creeds and confessions. However, those who investigate the matter seeking to please the Lord alone, will find that the *Westminster Confession* is the most Biblical. For expositions of the *Confession*, see Shaw ([1845] 1980) and Williamson (1964). Interestingly, the Assembly that wrote the *Confession* was called together by a civil government for the express purpose of composing a creed that would be used not only by the church, but also by the state. For more information on this see Hetherington ([1856] 1991, 122ff).

# CHAPTER THREE

## THE BIBLICAL CASE FOR AN ESTABLISHMENT OF RELIGION

Philosophical considerations alone should not be considered sufficient to prove that an establishment of religion *is* a moral obligation. For Christians only the Bible can be accepted as the foundation for any belief, not only those beliefs related to "spiritual" matters, but also those related to political issues. The critical question, then, for Christians is, "Does the Bible teach the necessity of the establishment of the Christian religion?" The Bible does indeed demonstrate the need for an establishment of Christianity, and the Old Testament in particular provides the Biblical basis for the concept of an established church. In Old Testament times there was a pervasive cooperation between church and state, and that pattern was *not* abrogated in the New Testament.

In the New Testament the passage with the most explicit teaching on civil government is probably Romans 13. In that chapter it is explained that political rulers "are ordained of God" (v. 1); "they are God's ministers" (v. 6) who must reward good and punish evil (vv. 3-4). This raises an important question: by what standard is the ruler to distinguish "good" from "evil"? Clearly, that standard can only be the Bible. How can rulers be God's ministers and yet not rule according to God's will? In other words, Romans 13: 1-6 teaches not only that God has instituted civil government, but also that the rulers must govern according to the Word of God. The Bible is not only the exclusive rule of faith and practice for the church, *but also for the state*. With the Bible being the standard for the civil authorities, it is unmistakable that Christianity is the foundation of the law order, i.e., the established religion in this sense. Romans 13, then, at least in a general way, teaches the necessity of the establishment of Christianity.

At this point it is important to be more specific about what is being proposed as the Biblical concept of established religion. The Bible teaches a cooperation between church and state that has been variously called the "Scottish Theory of Ecclesiastical Establishments" (Smeaton 1875), the "Establishment Principle" (Brown n.d., 1), and other similar terms.

> The Establishment Principle, or the Principle of the National Recognition of Religion maintains the scriptural view of the universal supremacy of Christ as King of Nations as well as King of saints, with the consequent duty of nations as such, and civil rulers in their official capacity, to honour and serve Him by

recognising His Truth and promoting His cause (Brown n.d., 1).

As William Cunningham explains it, "an obligation lies upon nations and their rulers to have respect, in the regulation of their national affairs, and in the application of national resources, to the authority of God's word, to the welfare of the church of Christ, and the interests of true religion" ([1882] 1991a, 391). What is being maintained here is that the true church of Christ, and the civil authorities (both in submission to their common Lord) have as their goal the promotion of God's glory and true Christianity, and that they should work together for the promotion of this common goal. On the one hand, they should be allied together, but on the other hand, they should remain completely sovereign in their respective jurisdictions.

Although this form of the establishment of Christianity is not explicity laid out in the New Testament, Symington finds the basic principle for it in Ephesians 1:22.

> Does not the apostle Paul speak of God having put all things under the feet of Christ, and 'given him to be Head over all things to the church?' Mark the language. It is not only 'Head over *all* things;' but 'Head over all things *to the Church*.' It is for the sake of the Church that he is invested with universal regal

authority: in other words, the *end* of Christ's universal Mediatorial dominion is *the good of the Church*. Thus far, all is clear and undeniable. But *the nations* are among the 'all things,' over which Christ is appointed 'Head.' It follows, then, that Christ is appointed *Head over the nations for the good of the Church*. If so, there must be some way in which the nations are capable of subserving the interests of the Church. Is it possible, then, to conceive that it is not the duty of the nations to promote, by every means in their power, the good of the Church? Is it conceivable that nations are not under obligations to advance the very end for which they are placed in subjection to Christ? Believe this who can ([1884] 1990, 266).

More specifically, however, the Biblical basis for the alliance between church and state is found in the Old Testament. As Smeaton notes, the Biblical authority for the Establishment Principle "will be found in the provisions of the Jewish Establishment, the existence of which, by Divine appointment, is conclusive as to the lawfulness of this arrangement" (1875, 7). The fact that so much of the detail for this arrangement is based on the Old Testament should not concern any Reformed Christians. Reformed theology recognizes the continuing validity of Old Testament laws and principles that have *not* been abrogated by the New Testament.

We must assume continuity with the Old Testament rather than discontinuity. This is *not* to say that there are *no changes* from Old to New Testament. Indeed, there are—important ones. However, the word of God must be the standard which defines precisely what those changes are for us; we cannot take it upon ourselves to assume such changes or read them into the New Testament. God's word, His direction to us, must be taken as continuing in its authority until God Himself reveals otherwise. This is, in a sense, the heart of "covenant theology" over against a dispensational understanding of the relation between Old and New Testaments (Bahnsen 1985, 3).

With this being the case, those who would argue against the Establishment Principle must show how the type of relationship which existed between the church and state in Old Testament Israel can no longer be a proper pattern because of changes made in the New Testament. This is not to suggest that a Christian society will simply be a carbon copy of Old Testament Israel. Rather, it is the underlying principle of a cooperative relationship between church and state that is still applicable. As M'Crie points out, those who claim that the Jewish Establishment "was altogether peculiar and inimitable do err, as well as those who hold that it is in all respects a model for Christian nations" (1871, 127). He suggests that there is a "golden mean" between these two positions.

Those who have read the Old Testament are well aware of the close connection between the Israelite church and state. Symington points out that

> at every stage of the Jewish history we meet
> two distinguished characters, the one civil and
> the other sacred, acting together a conspicuous
> part, and exhibiting the most perfectly harmonious
> co-operation. Such were Moses and Aaron, Joshua
> and Eleazar, David and Abiathar, Solomon and Zadok,
> Hezekiah and Azariah, Zerubbabel and Joshua ([1884]
> 1990, 272).

Of course, there are many more specific Scriptural examples of the alliance between church and state in the Old Testament. Those who would like a detailed study of this relationship should read *Aaron's Rod Blossoming* by George Gillespie ([1646] 1985). It is suffient for this book to acknowledge the general principle of cooperation between those two institutions.

> It is a striking fact, in confirmation of the views already
> laid down, that the only form of civil polity ever
> framed and established by God Himself should stand
> markedly in connection with the Church of God; and
> that although many of the circumstances attending
> the alliance of Church and state among the Jews were
> peculiar to that people, yet the alliance itself cannot be
> regarded as ceremonial or peculiar, but must be held as
> intimating the Divine will as to the lawfulness of such

a connection. Add to this fact that, beyond the case of the Jews, we have express support, and otherwise, to the Church of God by heathen magistrates, and the deed so done sanctioned by the approbation of God. Still further, this evidence of the Divine sanction given to the support and recognition of the Church by the state might be very greatly augmented by a consideration of those predictions in regard to the future or millennial state of the Church, in which kings and kingdoms are especially represented as in the latter days bringing their gold and their honour unto it, and becoming the great instruments of promoting its spiritual interests. Nor is the doctrine of the duty of the state to recognise and aid the Church invalidated by the absence of an express command in the New Testament Scriptures, confirmatory of the duty as announced in the Old. On the contrary, the absence of an express *prohibition* repealing the law, and superseding the principles acted on in Old Testament times, is the strongest of all evidence that the doctrine and duty remain the same as before (Bannerman [1869] 1991, 133).

Such is the thrust of the Biblical argument for the Establishment Principle.

It should be again noted that the Establishment Principle does not in any way allow for either the church or state to be in authority over the other in their respective God-given domains. The state cannot interfere in the affairs of the church, and the church cannot interfere in the affairs of the state. Thus each institution remains sovereign over the area granted to it by the Lord Jesus Christ. However, Gillespie notes that in very extraordinary circumstances, very extraordinary measures are called for. For example, if the church was to turn completely away from God "and their [sic] being no hopes of redressing such enormities in the ordinary way, by intrinsical ecclesiastical remedies" then "the Christian magistrate may and ought to interpose his authority to do divers things which, in an ordinary course of government, he ought not to do" ([1646] 1985, 82). There are a number of examples where various kings of Israel took the lead in reforming the church to turn it back to God. As John Knox concludes after examining the reformations wrought by King Hezekiah and King Josiah, "it is evident that the reformation of religion in all points, together with the punishment of false teachers, doth appertain to the power of the civil magistrate" ([1558] 1994, 90).

It is also important to note that the Establishment Principle does not lead to the creation of a totalitarian system. Although this will be dealt with more fully in the next chapter, a quotation from Symington expresses the point here very well.

> It is quite a mistake to say, that the magistrate's giving his countenance to one set of religious opinions

in preference to others, involves the essence of persecution. This arises from supposing that, when the government of a country expresses its approbation of a certain doctrinal creed and form of worship, it must forth with enjoin on all its subjects conformity in their opinions and practice, and authoritatively require the subjects to believe as the rulers believe. But does this follow? The legislature does not, in any sense, dictate to the subject what his religion shall be. It only determines what system of religious belief shall be taught with the aid and countenance of the state. No means but what are moral are employed to bring the public mind into conformity with that of the rulers. Every man is left, as far as civil authority or legal coercion is concerned, to choose or reject as he sees fit. The conscience of every individual is left free and unfettered; no one has the slightest ground on which to set up the cry of persecution ([1884] 1990, 288- 289).

The fear that some may have that the Establishment Principle will lead to a totalitarian government is therefore unfounded.

As has been shown in this chapter, the Establishment Principle is simply the Biblical pattern for church-state relations when both church and state are determined to serve the Lord. But it inevitably raises concerns about "liberty of conscience" and "toleration". Therefore these concerns are dealt with in the next chapter.

# CHAPTER FOUR

## RELIGIOUS LIBERTY, TOLERATION, AND THE ESTABLISHMENT OF CHRISTIANITY

As one would expect, the idea of an established religion automatically raises the question of other religions and dissenting beliefs. Would people of other religions or different Christian sects be allowed to freely exercise their beliefs? Since political beliefs are fundamentally based on religious beliefs, this question also applies to political ideas. Although advocates of the Establishment Principle might have some small differences among themselves regarding the degree to which liberty would be allowed, there is a basic principle upon which all would agree.

That principle is best summarized in the *Westminster Confession of Faith*, Chapter 20, "Of Christian Liberty, and Liberty of Conscience." Section 4 reads,

> And because the powers which God hath ordained, and the liberty which Christ hath purchased, are not intended by God to destroy, but mutually to uphold

and preserve one another; they who, upon pretence of Christian liberty, shall oppose any lawful power, or the lawful exercise of it, whether it be civil or ecclesiastical, resist the ordinance of God. And for their publishing of such opinions, or maintaining of such practices, as are contrary to the light of nature, or to the known principles of Christianity, whether concerning faith, worship, or conversation; or to the power of godliness; or such erroneous opinions or practices, as either in their own nature, or in the manner of publishing or maintaining them, are destructive to the external peace and order which Christ hath established in the church; they may lawfully be called to account, and proceeded against by the censures of the church, and by the power of the civil magistrate.

All sound Christians recognize that the civil government must govern according to the Word of God. God is the one who determines what are crimes and what are not. Many crimes are actions by people against other people. But it must also be recognized that the Scriptures teach that the civil government must also punish crimes that are committed against God, and against a law order based on God's Word. Thus idolatry and blasphemy are crimes as much as murder or theft. All 10 commandments, not just those that deal with interpersonal relations, are to be enforced by the state.

Although idolatry appears to be a crime that is committed exclusively against God, it is not. Since a Christian society would be based upon belief in the true God and His Word, idolatry actually undercuts the basis of a Christian society.

> Basic to the health of a society is the integrity of its foundation. To allow tampering with its foundation is to allow its total subversion. Biblical law can no more permit the propagation of idolatry than Marxism can permit counter-revolution, or monarchy a move to execute the king, or a republic an attempt to destroy the republic and create a dictatorship (Rushdoony 1973, 38-39).

Aside from the philosophical argument, there are explicit Scriptural prohibitions against idolatry, and explicit punishments for those who lead others away from the true God.

> It should be noted that Deuteronomy 13: 5-18 does not call for the death penalty for unbelief or for heresy. It condemns false prophets (vv. 1-5) who seek to lead the people, with signs and wonders, into idolatry. It does condemn individuals who secretly try to start a movement into idolatry (vv. 6-11). It does condemn cities which establish another religion and subvert the law-order of the nation (vv. 13-18), and this condemnation must be enforced by man to turn away the judgment of God (v. 17) (Rushdoony 1973, 39).

No Christian government can ignore what the Bible says regarding what might be termed "religious crimes". This part of God's Law is just as authoritative as the parts that deal with crimes of people against other people. As Samuel Rutherford puts it, the civil ruler is "to preserve both tables of the law" ([1644] 1982, 142), i.e., all ten of the commandments (Exodus 20: 1 - 17; Deuteronomy 5: 6 - 21).

It should also be pointed out that the section of the *Westminster Confession* quoted above was written specifically to counter abuses concerning "liberty of conscience." True Presbyterians have always defended every person's liberty of conscience. But here the Confession states that liberty of conscience cannot be used as an excuse to oppose "lawful power" and to disturb "the external peace and order" of the church. Liberty of conscience does not override the obligation to obey authorities acting according to God's Word. "He who is the Lord of the conscience has also instituted the authorities in Church and State; and it would be in the highest degree absurd to suppose that he has planted in the breast of every individual a power to resist, counteract, and nullify his own ordinances" (M'Crie [1821] 1989, 162).

Nevertheless, there will likely be those who will allege that the *Confession* is here granting the civil government almost unlimited power to oppress and persecute its citizens. Some will maintain, "whenever government officials discover anyone who makes statements with which they disagree, the police will be sent out and those persons will be silenced." In other words, the *Confession* is basically advocating a totalitarian state. However, this is not, in fact, the kind of state power for which the *Confession* is calling. The Scottish theologian, Thomas M'Crie, gave a clear exposition of this section of the *Confession*, in response to the type of criticism mentioned above. The following lengthy quotation will lay that criticism to rest.

> Now, this does not say that all who publish such opinions and maintain such practices (as are here mentioned) may be proceeded against, or, punished (if the substitution of this word shall be insisted for) by the civil magistrate; nor does it say, that any good and peaceable subject shall be made liable to this process simply on the ground of religious opinions published and practices maintained by him. For, in the *first* place, persons of a particular character are spoken of in this paragraph, and these are very different from good and peaceable subjects. They are described in the former sentence as "they who *oppose* lawful power or the lawful exercise of it," and "*resist* the ordinance of God." The same persons are spoken of in the sentence under consideration, as appears from the copulative and relative. It is not said, "*Any one* for publishing," etc.,

but "they who *oppose* any lawful power, etc. for *their* publishing," etc.

In the *second* place, this sentence specifies some of the ways in which these persons may become chargeable with the opposition mentioned, and consequently "*may* be called to account;" but it does not assert that even they must or ought to be prosecuted for every avowed opinion or practice of the kind referred to. . . . For, be it observed, it is not the design of the paragraph to state the objects of church censure or civil prosecution; its proper and professed object is to interpose a check on the abuse of liberty of conscience as operating to the prejudice of just and lawful authority. It is not sin *as sin*, but as *scandal*, or injurious to the spiritual interests of Christians, that is the proper object of church censure; and it is not for sins as such, but for *crimes*, that persons become liable to punishment by magistrates. The compilers of the Confession were quite aware of these distinctions, which were then common. . . . To render an action the proper object of magisterial punishment, it is not enough that it be contrary to the law of God, whether natural or revealed; it must, in one way or another, strike against the public good of society ([1821] 1989, 163-164).

Chapter 20 of the *Westminster Confession* is a statement promoting the Christian doctrine of "liberty of conscience" and section 4 was not included to cancel out the rest of the chapter. The *Confession* does genuinely allow for liberty of conscience. But liberty of conscience is not absolute. Just as the state has limitations placed on its authority and power, so also the individual has limitations placed on his promotion of opinions and practices. As Bannerman states, the object of the *Confession*'s "authors was accomplished in announcing the general doctrine that there are such limits, and that there are such opinions and practices; thereby contradicting the mischievous tenet, that conscience is a plea sufficient against the lawful exercise of all authority whatsoever" ([1869] 1991, 184). However, "[w]here those limits are to be laid down, it is not at all the object of the Confession to say. At *what point* the plea of conscience ceases to avail against the interference of authority, whether civil or ecclesiastical, our Confession does not profess to determine" (Bannerman [1869] 1991, 184).

That the *Confession*'s authors felt it necessary to write out a statement expressing the limitations on liberty of conscience is understandable considering the historical situation in which they lived. At the time, England was experiencing a civil war and certain sectarian groups were using "liberty of conscience" as a slogan to advocate various forms of lawlessness.

> The Sectaries who during the civil wars used the watchwords of "liberty of conscience" and "universal toleration," in behalf of views which the authors of the

Westminster standards felt bound to oppose as in the highest degree destructive of civil and ecclesiastical order, may be divided into four classes: 1. Those who "pretended liberty of conscience" against all Church authority,—such as the Brownists, who held that no man should be brought under Church discipline or excommunicated for any action or opinion in behalf of which he could urge that plea. 2. Those who "pretended liberty of conscience" against all civil authority,—such as the Fifth Monarchy men, who demanded universal community of goods and levelling of ranks, and "the world to be put under the feet of the saints." 3. Those who "pretended liberty of conscience" against the practical authority of the law of God,—such as the Antinomians, who maintained that the moral law was buried in the grave of Christ, and was no longer binding upon a Christian man as a rule of duty. 4. Those who "pretended liberty of conscience" against the authority of God as a standard of belief conveyed to us in the Scriptures,—such as the Libertines, who asserted that all opinions were alike innocent, if only held conscientiously (Bannerman [1869] 1991, 182-183).

These views were expressed in "dangerous and often most blasphemous and repulsive forms" thus making it necessary for the *Confession*'s authors to strongly oppose such a false use of "liberty of conscience". The demand for "toleration" was closely linked with the concept of "liberty of conscience" at the time the *Confession* was being written. In discussing "toleration" as the sectarians defined it, Hetherington gives a description not unlike the quote from Bannerman above.

> As used by those military sectarians, the meaning of the term ["toleration"] was, that any man might freely utter the ravings of his own heated fancy, and endeavour to proselytise others, be his opinions what they might,—even though manifestly subversive of all morality, all government, and all revelation. Such a toleration, for instance, as would include alike Antinomians and Anabaptists, though teaching that they were set free from and above the rules of moral duty so completely, that to indulge in the grossest licentiousness was in them no sin; and Levellers and Fifth-Monarchy Men, whose tenets went directly to the subversion of every kind of constituted government, and all distinctions in rank and property. This was what *they* meant by *toleration*,—and this was what the Puritans and Presbyterians condemned and wrote against with startled vehemence ([1856] 1991, 154).

By understanding what the *Confession*'s authors were up against at the time of the Assembly, we can more accurately discern the meaning they intended for Section 4 of Chapter 20.

It should be clear now that under a Presbyterian Establishment there will be some form of liberty of conscience, namely, that which is stated in Chapter 20 of the *Westminster Confession of Faith*. Liberty of conscience is limited, and cannot be used to justify the promotion of idolatry or wickedness. Hetherington summarizes the presbyterian understanding of liberty of conscience this way:

> The Word of God, in almost innumerable instances, commands the direct encouragement of truth, and also the suppression of certain *forms* of error,—as of idolatry and blasphemy; but gives no authority to man to judge and punish errors of the mind, so far as these amount not to violations of known and equitable laws, and disturb not the peace of society ([1856] 1991, 330).

With regards to "errors of the mind," William Cunningham too writes that "civil rulers . . . must not inflict upon men civil pains and penalties,—fines, imprisonment, or death,—merely on account of differences of opinion upon religious subjects" ([1882] 1991b, 562). Robert Shaw agrees with this as well.

> All sound Presbyterians disclaim all intolerant or compulsory measures with regard to matters purely religious. They maintain that no man should be punished or molested on account of his religious opinions or observances, provided there is nothing in these hurtful to the general interests of society, or

dangerous to the lawful institutions of the country in which he lives ([1845] 1980, 210).

And Thomas M'Crie also points out that in discharging their duties the civil rulers will not be "compelling their subjects to believe or practice what they do not believe or judge sinful" and will not be "punishing persons who may conscientiously dissent from the authorised and established religion, or depriving them of their natural rights merely on this ground" (1871, 83). He adds that rulers are not "warranted forcibly to impose a profession of faith upon their subjects, or to oblige them to worship God in a certain mode, under civil penalties to be inflicted upon all who dissent or refuse compliance" (1871, 148).

Presbyterianism is Biblical Christianity, and a Presbyterian civil government will be nothing more than civil government conducted strictly according to the Bible. Thus justice will be defined by God and guided by the Scriptures. Those "religious crimes" which God says must be punished, will be punished, and in the way God stipulates. However, this does not mean that people will be forced to believe in God and proper doctrine. The Bible also limits the power of the state in dealing with unbelievers. Just as "strangers" were allowed to live under the civil government of Old Testament Israel, so also they will be allowed to live in a society under true Presbyterian civil government. Rushdoony describes the situation of the stranger.

God's law repeatedly refers to the stranger and requires particular recognition of their [sic] freedom. They are not to be oppressed, and discrimination against them is forbidden. "One law shall be to him that is homeborn, and unto the stranger that sojourneth among you" (Ex.12:49). This law was given to Israel in Egypt, before their departure, to stress the fact that justice is without respect of persons. The protection of the law must extend to aliens: "Ye shall have one manner of law, as well for the stranger, as for one of your own country: for I am the LORD your God" (Lev. 24:22; Num. 15:15,16). Racial or national differences could not be used to bar aliens from knowledge of God's law, nor from the Passover (Num.9:14; Deut. 31:10-12; Josh. 8:34f.). Because the foreigner, if not seeking admission into the covenant, had another religion, he was not required to abide by the ritual laws the covenant requires. He could enter into long-term debt, for example (Deut.15:3; cf. 23:21), and disregard the dietary laws (Deut. 14:21). The foreigner could not ascend Israel's throne (Deut. 17:15). However, his status was that of a privileged guest (1986, 63).

Since the strangers were under the exact same law as the Israelites themselves, and were yet allowed to live in the land while not being believers, it is clear that the enforcement of God's Law by the civil government cannot and will not lead to the extermination of non-Christians. Sure there are limitations on liberty of conscience, but there are also limitations on the state.

This can best be summed up with another quotation from Bannerman.

> The truth is, that those two ordinances of God—that of civil authority on the one side, and that of conscience on the other—cannot be inconsistent with or destructive of each other. They are designed for concert and co-operation, not for conflict or mutual destruction. Those disciples of toleration who would plead liberty of conscience as an argument to justify resistance to civil authority in its lawful exercise, are wrong. Those disciples of despotism who would plead the authority of civil government in order to set aside or overbear the rights of conscience, are equally wrong. Civil government on the one hand, and conscience on the other, are alike ordinances of God, and were appointed to act in harmony with each other; and that they *may act* in harmony, they must *limit* each other. Civil authority is not absolute or unlimited; for there is a point where in its exercise it meets with the rightful domain of conscience; and the sword ought to be sheathed, and to give way before the claims which conscience pleads. Conscience, on the other hand, is not absolute or unlimited either; for there is a point where its rights are met and bounded by the rights of civil authority ([1869] 1991, 168- 169).

# CHAPTER FIVE

## CONCLUSION

It is hoped that this book has demonstrated the necessity of the establishment of Christianity in general, and presbyterianism in particular, as the official religion of every society. Every society is based on an established religion, and therefore Bible-believing Christians must, of course, advocate that true Christianity be the established religion in whichever country they live. To not advocate the establishment of the one true religion is a violation of the first commandment as it applies to the state (cf. *Westminster Larger Catechism* questions 103-105). Furthermore, Christianity must be defined in order to distinguish it from the many "Christian" sects that offer erroneous alternatives to true Biblical Christianity, i.e., Presbyterianism. The Scriptures also give us a pattern of church-state cooperation that is not only still valid, but represents the only pattern for civil government that has been endorsed by God Himself. However, fears that this would involve the creation of a totalitarian state are unfounded. The state is obligated to enforce the Law of God and cannot go beyond that Law since it is limited by the very Law that spells out its responsibilities.

Undoubtedly, the Establishment Principle is a very foreign and unsettling concept for the modern mind. Even among Bible-believing Christians, the idea of a separation of church and state is adhered to strongly. Yet this book represents an appeal to go back to Scripture to see what type of relationship God requires between these two institutions. Both church and state are ordained by God to serve Him and promote His glory. They are to work together to achieve those ends.

It is not likely that the ideas promoted here will become widely acceptable in the near future. They are too foreign to the predominating viewpoints of modern times. But some words from Gary North are appropriate here.

> I am not writing a manifesto to be used in today's elections. I am writing a manifesto for the more distant future. I realize that a Christian politician or activist who is living on this side of the looming crises, and on this side of the great work of the Holy Spirit, will probably prefer to disassociate himself from these sentiments (1989, 658).

In time, when the millennial blessings spoken of in the Scriptures come to pass, the Establishment Principle will once again become the basis of Christian concepts of civil government. Hopefully this book will, in some small way, contribute to making the Establishment Principle acceptable again.

In the immediate future, Christians should be concerned about the issues that are currently facing our nations. Although the Establishment Principle is very important, it is not part of today's political discourse, and will not be until more Christians begin to see its necessity. In the meantime, political activism must continue to be directed to the pressing issues of the day. Greg Bahnsen made an important comment regarding the theoretical aspects of Scriptural teaching on political matters and the imperative of dealing with current issues. When asked "Should we execute idolaters?", he responded,

> The *prima facie* understanding of the biblical texts would seem to support the justice of punishing idolatry, even today. But I have not done sufficient homework and reflection on this question. Instead of talking about these theoretical things, we should work to end the slaughter of unborn children, our nation's widespread sexual perversion, and the state's continual intrusion into our lives by, for example, its stealing of our property and intervention in Christian schools. Let us talk to each other about these immediate, real situations first of all. As time goes on, we should together exegete key biblical passages about other important social problems. Killing idolaters is not the agenda (1989, 268).

Theoretical matters are important; indeed, this book is about the "theory" of Christian civil government. But it is also true that Christians should be dealing with contemporary issues such as the ongoing murder of unborn children. Even more importantly, Christians need to ensure that their own children are receiving a Christian education. Only by raising godly families and evangelizing the lost will the foundation be laid for the future reconstruction of civil government along Biblical lines.

May God be glorified, even in discussions about His will for politics and civil government!

# References

Bahnsen, Greg L. 1985. *By This Standard*. Tyler, Texas: Institute for Christian Economics.

Bahnsen, Greg L. 1989. "Questions Addressed to Greg L. Bahnsen." In *God and Politics*, ed. Gary Scott Smith. Phillipsburg, New Jersey: Presbyterian and Reformed Publishing Company.

Bannerman, James. [1869] 1991. *The Church of Christ*. Vol. 1. Edmonton, Alberta: Still Waters Revival Books.

Brown, C.J. N.d. *Christ's Kingship Over the Nations*. Gisborne, New Zealand: Westminster Standard.

Cunningham, William. [1882] 1991a. *Historical Theology*. Vol. 1. Edmonton, Alberta: Still Waters Revival Books.

Cunningham, William. [1882] 1991b. *Historical Theology*. Vol. 2. Edmonton, Alberta: Still Waters Revival Books.

Gillespie, George. [1646] 1985. *Aaron's Rod Blossoming*. Harrisonburg, Virginia: Sprinkle Publications.

Hetherington, William M. [1856] 1991. *History of the Westminster Assembly of Divines*. Edmonton, Alberta: Still Waters Revival Books.

Knox, John. [1558] 1994. "The Appellation of John Knox from the cruel and most injust sentence pronounced against him by the false bishops and clergy of Scotland, with his supplication and exhortation to the nobility, estates and commonalty of the same realm." In John Knox *On Rebellion*, ed. Roger A. Mason. Cambridge: Cambridge University Press.

Marshall, Paul. 1992. "Religion and Canadian Culture." In *Shaping a Christian Vision for Canada: Discussion Papers on Canada's Future*, ed. Aileen Van Ginkel. Markham, Ontario: Faith Today Publications.

M'Crie, Thomas. 1871. *Statement of the Difference Between the Profession of the Reformed Church of Scotland, as Adopted by Seceders, and the Profession Contained in the New Testimony and Other Acts Lately Adopted by the General Associate Synod*. Edinburgh: C.F. Lyon.

M'Crie, Thomas. [1821] 1989. *Unity of the Church*. Dallas, Texas: Presbyterian Heritage Publications.

North, Gary, 1989. *Political Polytheism*. Tyler, Texas: Institute for Christian Economics.

Rushdoony, Rousas John. [1968] 1978. *The Foundations of Social Order*. Fairfax, Virginia: Thoburn Press.

Rushdoony, Rousas John. 1973. *The Institutes of Biblical Law*. Phillipsburg, New Jersey: Presbyterian and Reformed Publishing Company.

Rushdoony, Rousas John. 1986. *Christianity and the State*. Vallecito, California: Ross House Books.

Rutherford, Samuel. [1644] 1982. *Lex, Rex*. Harrisonburg, Virginia: Sprinkle Publications.

Shaw, Robert. [1845] 1980. *An Exposition of the Confession of Faith*. Lochcarron, Scotland: Christian Focus Publications.

Smeaton, George. 1875. *The Scottish Theory of Ecclesiastical Establishments and How Far the Theory is Realised*. Glasgow: The Glasgow Conservative Association's Rooms.

Symington, William. [1884] 1990. *Messiah the Prince*. Edmonton, Alberta: Still Waters Revival Books.

Tallach, Ian R. 1980. "Publisher's Preface." In *An Exposition of the Confession of Faith*, by Robert Shaw. Lochcarron, Scotland: Christian Focus Publications.

Various Authors. [1647] 1983. *Westminster Confession of Faith*. Scotland: Free Presbyterian Publications.

Williamson, G.I. 1964. *The Westminster Confession of Faith for Study Classes*. Phillipsburg, New Jersey: Presbyterian and Reformed Publishing Company.

Printed in the United States
98483LV00004B/1-24/A

9 780978 098735